Project Management:

Secrets Successful Project Managers Know and What You Can Learn From Them

A Beginner's Guide to Project Management With Tips On Learning The Essential Soft Skills To Manage A Project Like A Pro

By

Bryan Oliver

Join the FLIGHT Crew and get our

monthly newsletter at

www.flight4success.com

Publisher: Flight4Success Publishers
Editor: Zain Hemani

Table of Contents

Introduction

Who is this Book for?

This book is meant for those who have little to no experience in project management and is by no means a replacement for the extensive study and art of project management. This book will address more of the art involved in project management, however, you will also get a high level overview of the phases of project management. At the back of the book you will find a glossary, so you have a reference of some of the most common used terms in project management.

What You Will Learn

This book is not a quick fix and does not replace the years of experience and study of the most seasoned and successful project managers.

However, there are some key skills and tips you need to learn when it comes to succeeding in a project management interview and dealing with your teams and stakeholders. If applied early and often, these skills can and will set you apart from the majority of project managers out there. Why? I'm so glad you asked. The reason is most likely focus. The field of project management is not easy and takes many years to become proficient. Most of the average project managers I've worked with over the years focus on the tactical and technical approaches to project management. The elite level project managers are experts at these approaches, but they take it a step further. They take the time to learn and implement these key skills where the average project manager will not take the time to educate themselves.

I've been managing projects and project managers for the better part of 17 years now and I have to say, my career has been extremely rewarding. If you are looking to get into project management or just starting out, you've come to the right place. You are embarking on an amazing journey which has some fantastic benefits. But, make no mistake, you will need to work hard and if you want to be one of the best you will need to do more than just learn to manage a project. I'm excited to share with you what I've learned from my own personal experiences and through the experiences of the many phenomenal project managers I've had the privilege of working with and serving over

the years.

What is a Project Manager and Why Companies Need You

According to Wikipedia, "a project manager is a professional in the field of project management. Project managers can have the responsibility of the planning, execution and closing of any project, typically relating to the construction industry, architecture, aerospace and defense, computer networking, telecommunications or software development". For executives of a company, the benefits of having a project manager are many, however the true value of a project manager comes in the form of cost savings, reduced risk, and improved success rates on projects.

What is a Project?

There are various interpretations and

definitions of what a project is. This book

defines a project with the following criteria:

- A project is temporary, meaning it has a

  predetermined beginning and end date.

- A project has a unique set of tasks,

  meaning what is performed during a

  project will not necessarily be done on

  an ongoing basis as part of a company's

  daily operations.

- Has a defined scope and specific set of

  resources to be used

Key Skills of a Project Manager

Over the years, I have worked with and interviewed hundreds of project managers. The best ones I've worked with are experts in the following areas:

Communication and building rapport

In every interview I conduct, I ask the following question, "What do you believe are the top 3 skills a project manager should have?" Of all the many different answers I get, the one I am always looking for is communication. I am ok if they don't say this first but they must speak about it, or the rest of the interview typically goes south. Being able to effectively communicate with your project teams and stakeholders is critical for the success of the project.

As a project manager you must be able to provide accurate and thorough updates to those that need to have information in order to make appropriate decisions. Unfortunately, sometimes you'll need to be the bearer of bad news. Your job as the project manager is to ensure any news or status is communicated and if something is wrong, you need to be able to communicate the mitigation plan. You can make the communication process easier by building a connection with your team and project sponsors.

One particular project manager I know takes the time to get to know each individual on her team before the project kicks off. If she is in the same office, she sets up an in person meeting to further build a connection. By doing this, she learns what is important to them and where their roadblocks and challenges exist. You'd be surprised how often project managers sit behind their computers and only communicate with their team via email, instant message, and the occasional conference call, rarely taking the time to build a relationship with team members or those paying for the project.

Pro Tip: When getting to know your team members, ask them about previous projects and where the major "gotchas" were. By doing this, you are showing them that you respect and value their experience and you are there to help prevent the pain points they previously experienced. People are more than willing to work with you at crunch time or go above and beyond when you need them to if they LIKE, TRUST, and RESPECT you.

Be Organized with Attention to Detail

Projects are comprised of many moving parts. In order to be effective, you'll need to be well organized and pay close attention to detail. Although having knowledge and experience may be a job requirement, it doesn't mean you will need to be an expert at specific project management software. If you are just beginning your project management job, the chances are you will not be required to have thorough knowledge of software like Microsoft Project. However, you will be expected to keep track of all pieces of the project and be able to provide status in any given area and at any given time. For this, you need to make sure you are well organized and are paying close attention to the details of project. Depending on the company, you will need to take the time to learn the budget, changes, and any project management systems that are in place. Some use out-of-box software, like MS Project and others have in-house systems. Your role and responsibility as a project manager is to be familiar with these systems and effectively utilize them in the manner your client requires.

Leadership

Leadership is a characteristic I often see missing in many project managers. There is a big difference between being part of a project and leading a project. To be effective and successful, project managers need to develop strong leadership skills.

What is a leader?

A leader does the following:

1) Inspires a vision for what the future will look like

2) Motivates the team to want to be part of that vision

3) Oversees the delivery and success of that vision

4) Coaches, mentors, and builds up the team to increase the effectiveness of executing the vision

Pro Tip: Understand that your team wants the project to succeed and they are looking to you to guide them to victory. Take every opportunity to motivate, encourage, and make a connection with your team. If they know you have their back, they will have yours.

Intuition

Intuition is a skill that is innate in everyone and to a certain degree, it cannot be coached. When it comes to project management, intuition is developed over time and through experience. Do you ever wonder how some people can anticipate something going wrong at work and prevent it from going too far? This is their intuition at play. If you are new in your career, you can practice this by trying to anticipate the next move in small areas of your project. Some of the best lessons you will learn to build your intuition will come from making mistakes. Don't let these mistakes discourage you. It's part of the process and you need to learn from it and adjust accordingly. In order to be at the top of your game, you need to work on developing this skill.

🔅 **Pro Tip:** Find senior project managers that are willing to mentor you. Ask them a lot of questions. You will begin to see a pattern in the way some of the best pick up on issues that may arise. Most people are willing to share their experiences, so utilize these great resources.

People Skills

This section is taken from the personality styles section of my book _Habits: Create What You Need To Succeed In Life_. This skill and habit will not only set you apart from other project managers, but it will serve as a strong foundation for your future career success. I cannot emphasize enough how much positive impact this particular skill can have on your career.

Your personality related to how you tend to think, feel, and behave—is shaped by your genetic makeup as well as your life experiences. Our personalities determine the way we interact with people in our life. Understanding the power of our personality will help prepare us to attain success.

Part of being a successful and competent individual in the workplace is to know your strengths, weaknesses, communication skills, and learning styles. There are many excellent personality assessments that can assist you with discovering more about yourself. As you learn more about your own personality type, it is imperative that you learn more about the personality types of others.

There are four basic personality types. Depending on the personality test you take, the names may be different. The four main personality types are:

1. Type A

2. Analytical

3. Feeler

4. Expressive

People who are Type A tend to focus on fact rather than emotion. They are driven to see measurable results, and their intensity may make them quick to offend people, even though that may not be their intention. Type A personalities like to act quickly and are enthusiastic about tackling projects and seeing results. If you want something done, call a person with a Type A personality.

Analytical personalities like to amass details and comb through them first rather than acting hastily. They value accuracy in their work and expect the same precision and excellence from others. They relate to Ben Franklin's motto, "Everything has a place and everything in its place."

People with Feeler personalities are people-centric and value meaningful relationships. This personality style makes for great team players, as people with this personality type are patient and want to interact with their coworkers on a personal level. They are revealing when it comes to the events of their life, hope to know others, and are sensitive to the feelings of others. If you need someone to talk to, go find someone with the Feeler personality. They can talk through issues with you and are willing to help if they can.

Those with Expressive personalities are creative and astute in the art of persuasion. Because they are enthusiastic and friendly, expressive personality people value communicating with others and thrive when the lines of communication are open. Expressive personalities long for recognition and often need support to reign in their many ideas in order to achieve specific goals.

It is important to remember that no one person fits perfectly into one category. Each individual is likely to express characteristics that are indicative to all four types, with a greater emphasis on one or two. These categories are not meant to put people into behavioral boxes. Instead, they are meant to help us better understand each other's tendencies. These characteristics can help us understand the deeper motivations of each member on your team, including the most important person, yourself.

To understand your own personality and where you tend to lean, consider taking an in-depth personality test like Myers-Briggs or

Strengthsfinder 2.0. Learning your personality type will be an ongoing process and study for the remainder of your career. Once you've gained a basic framework of your personality, the next step is to learn about the other three styles and how they work together. As a leader of your projects, you will need to understand your team's personality style and tendencies in order to get the most value for the project.

Pro Tip: Become an expert on your personality style and start to identify others with a similar style. After that, you can do a deep dive into the other personalities and learn the nuances and gifts each person brings to the team.

Emotional Intelligence

IQ is often talked about relative to how smart and successful someone is. Less talked about, but just as to the success in project management is emotional intelligence (EQ). Your EQ is measured by how well you are aware of and in control of your emotions. Having a high EQ allows you to adapt quickly, and empathize with your project team and stakeholders. High EQ also allows you to overcome obstacles which are sure to arise in your project, and deal with conflict management. Let's take a look at these situations in a little more detail.

Projects change and evolve daily, and sometimes hourly. Your success will depend on your ability to adapt to these constant changes. Remember that you will be faced with unforeseeable obstacles and there will be people on your team with their own agendas as well. It is important that you weed out any conflicts and align with those who share your vision and the end goal of the project. All this will be going on while you are motivating and guiding your team to the finish line. To become the best project manager, you must become an expert in managing all these areas. In order to do that, you must look for ways to increase your emotional intelligence. I will provide a couple of good book references for you at the end of this book should you decide to go into a deeper study on emotional intelligence.

Pro Tip: Make it a practice to not immediately respond or participate in a heated email or instant message debate. If you disagree with something you are reading, wait 24 hours, formulate your answer in an unemotional state, then respond. Emotionally responding to any form of communication, especially in email, has the potential to severely limit your career potential – yes, read this as 'get yourself fired'.

Customer Service

This is probably one of the key areas I see many project managers fall short on. Many of us are very process driven and have an incredible ability to drive a project through the project phases to closure on time and on budget. While this is fantastic, some forget whom they are working for and the reason they are employed. "But who is the customer?" you might be asking yourself. Always remember that your stakeholder is your customer. While it is true that your stakeholder is your end customer, keep in mind that there are many other people you will be dealing with.

For example, I contend that your team is also your customer and that you are there to serve them. The thing you need to remember is that without your team, your project will not get done. I've seen many project managers take the approach of pounding the table and pushing for performance with no regard for those on the team. Most of these folks don't last very long in their roles. On the flip side, I've seen some project managers provide some amazing customer service and they have a team that will go the distance for them. As a by-product of this behavior, their projects are successfully completed and the stakeholders come back with more work. Can you see the difference here? You can literally create longevity in your career by providing exceptional customer service.

💡 ***Pro Tip:*** View each of your team members as your customer. Look for ways you can exceed their expectations and provide better service to them.

Influence

As a project manager, you will typically not have anyone that directly reports to you. Rather, you will be managing resources that are part of the organization. These resources have their own managers and are working on other projects, in addition to yours. In other words, you will need to influence without authority.

In order to effectively complete your project, you will need to influence the resources on your team to do what is needed for the project. Sometimes, this will come at a time when they have competing priorities. We previously spoke about Emotional Intelligence, and this is where this skill comes into play. You must be fully aware of the situation your resources are in, have empathy, and look for ways to help them succeed; not only in your project but in their other projects as well. By showing them you understand their situation and you are empathetic toward them, you stand a good chance at gaining their loyalty.

Pro Tip: Get to know your teams outside of the work they do. What are their hobbies? Do they have children? You can better influence someone when you know and understand their personal wants, needs and desires.

Stakeholder Management

A stakeholder is someone that has a vested interest in the project you are leading. Managing your stakeholders is as much of an art as it is a skill. There will be some stakeholders that will want early and often communication while others just want high level updates once or every other week. It is up to you to ask them how often they'd like communication and to what level. While this sounds like a fairly simple task, you'd be surprised how many project managers fail in this area. My belief is they fail because they assume all stakeholders are alike and receive information in the same way. Some will want very detailed updates while others just want to know if the project is on track and if there are any issues or risks. Assuming all stakeholders want the same things may cause you to be viewed as ineffective in the eyes of some. Unfortunately, you will not please everyone, but you do need to understand those that need pleasing and communicate accordingly.

Pro Tip: Identify early which stakeholders will be your allies and which will be your opponents. In larger projects, you will find some stakeholders who have their own agendas, and your project is not one of their priorities. As a matter of fact, you may have a stakeholder who wants your project to fail, so they can highlight and provide credence to something on their

agenda.

Conflict Management

If you are running a project, you will experience

conflict. It may be directed at you or you may

have conflict within the team. Either way,

developing the skills to effectively manage

conflict will move your project along and could

potentially save it from a disastrous failure.

Understanding the personality styles and

building those relationships early on will help

you when conflict arises.

Pro Tip: When conflict arises, don't try to

exert your authority in a public setting. This will

only serve to put the person in conflict on the

defensive and make them want to prove their

point further. Instead, set up some time with

the person or persons, in private, and discuss

the issue at hand. It may take a little extra time,

but you will find it will save you significant time

and aggravation later.

Getting the Job

Interviewing Skills

I am not going to bore you with interviewing

tips you can glean from the thousands of

websites out there. What I will provide are

three things I look for when I'm interviewing

someone and what I have found to be

consistent with those that perform the best

after they are hired. I have worked with and

interviewed hundreds of project managers over

the last 15 years. The ones that have left the

strongest impressions mastered the following

three tips.

Tip #1 Tell the Story before You're Asked

When I'm interviewing a potential candidate, I have a few expectations, which I don't share upfront. One of those expectations is that the candidate will answer some of my questions before I ever ask them and the more senior the project manager, the more detail I expect them to provide.

Here's an example. A common question in an interview goes something like, "Tell me about your experience." Before you interview do your homework on the types of questions that are typically asked of a project manager and address those questions in your story about your experience. The more experience you have, the more detailed your explanations will be. If you have little to no experience, draw information from your part time jobs, school projects, or volunteering to shape your story and answer questions you might be asked. It's rare but I've had interviews where I asked the candidate just one question and they answered the rest of my questions in the story. Needless to say, I recommended the person for hire immediately.

Tip #2 Make Your Weaknesses Your Strengths

A common question that is asked in an interview, especially when you have little to no experience, is, "Tell me about your strengths and weaknesses." You can effectively answer this question by discussing your weaknesses and showing the interviewer how you've turned that weakness into a strength. Everyone has weaknesses so you might as well figure out what yours are and learn to make them your strengths. On top of this, explain how you have applied this strength so they see you in action.

Here is an example. Let's say one of your weaknesses is lack of organization. I know what you're thinking, you'd never tell an interviewer that you lack organization skills. You can, however, turn this into a positive trait because you've taken the time to overcome this weakness and taken the time to create a new strength. You can say something like this; 'one of my weaknesses, which is now become one of my strengths or greatest assets, is lack of organization. I found that I was taking on too much work and becoming unorganized. Because of this, I decided to implement a strategy where today I am highly organized and efficient in my work'. You see how you've shown your weakness and also demonstrated how you've turned it into a strength? Be prepared to elaborate on the strategy should you be asked for more details.

Tip # 3 Be Interested in Them

We all listen to the same radio station WIIFM –
What's in it for me. In an interview, it's your job
to relate to the interviewer and not the other
way around. Consider the interviewer as the
gate keeper to the company you are trying to
join. They have their own interests and what
they care about, so make sure you understand
what they are.

You can do this by taking an honest and sincere
interest in them and their company. A great
way to kill your interview is if you are asked,
"Tell me what you know about our company,"
and you either give some generic answer or
speak out some quotes from their website.
Here's a secret for you. The last 10 people they

interviewed said the same thing. Really learn about the company and learn about the interviewer. Understand the company's position in the market place, who their competitors are, and what their differentiator is. If you can't find that information on the internet, those are good questions for you to ask when you are given the opportunity.

Also, you will often be given the name(s) of the people that will be interviewing you. You can head over to LinkedIn and learn about them. Not that you want to stalk them but you can learn more about them on Facebook and other social media sites. Don't think for a minute they are not checking out your social media footprint. If the company is truly a good fit for you, there will be common interests and

interesting facts you will want to know about.

After all, you will be spending 40 plus hours a

week with these people, so you want to make

sure you like them and vice versa.

Doing the Job – Phases of a Project

The following is an overview of the phases of a project. It is by no means, meant to be an all-inclusive list. If you are just starting out as a project manager or looking to get into project management, this chapter will provide some key items you will need to know in order to successfully manage a project. If you are looking to further study the field of project management, the Project Management Institute is a great place to start. There are also hundreds of websites for you to gain some insight. Although there is no substitute for experience to really learn how these phases work on a daily basis, gaining a high level understanding and applying the

aforementioned skills, will go a long way to

securing your future success.

Initiation

Before a project even begins, there is certain alignment that needs to occur between the stakeholders, those who are paying for the project. The first thing that happens is that an idea is presented. The idea will present the goals and scope of the project, the benefits to the organization, possible high level cost estimates, and potential risks for doing or not doing the project. Once the idea is presented, feasibility needs to be determined. Depending on the size of the project, feasibility may have already been done before the idea is presented, to strengthen the case of the proposal. Finally, the project will need stakeholder commitment.

Once the project is committed to, then you are

ready to begin planning.

Planning

The components of the planning phase will begin with the Project Charter. The project's charter will outline the scope of the project as well as provide assumptions and high level requirements. Also included in the project charter is a high level schedule overview which is an outline of the resources needed, project milestones, and a communication plan that will be used for the duration of the project. During this time, you will begin the project by inviting all the necessary resources you have found. Some organizations have resource assignment mechanisms that can help you determine who these individuals are. If you don't have such a mechanism and are part of a smaller organization, you will need to speak to your

department heads to determine if their

involvement may be needed.

Execution, Control and Monitoring

Once you have a plan for the project, it's time to begin execution. During the execution, you will be working on the Control and Monitoring phase at that same time. The first thing you will need to do is have a working session with your team and run through the schedule. Depending on the size of your team, you can do this as one large group or meet with each team member individually. I've done it both ways and the larger group has worked better for smaller projects.

As the work begins, you need to start a cadence of weekly team meetings and status reports so the stakeholders' have a good idea of where the project stands. In the status report, you'll need to include an overview of the project description, completed and upcoming milestones, any significant accomplishments, along with risks and issues. What you must understand when it comes to the status report is that your stakeholder, typically executives, will glance at your report for less than a minute. In a larger organization, the stakeholders are responsible for quite a number of projects and usually have very little time to go into the details. So, your job is to highlight the major components of the project in as short a space as possible. This includes providing enough detail so they understand any risks or issues and if they need to take any action.

Throughout the execution of the project, you need to monitor and control how the project is doing. Your job as a project manager, as I mentioned earlier, is to anticipate issues that may arise, act on them, and control the situation. This is done through active engagement with your project team. Often, this will occur on a weekly basis, but many times, depending on where you are in the project, you may need to speak to them daily and possibly even hourly. At the most basic level, however, you will need consistent updates from your team so you know where the project stands so you can assist your team to get them where they need to be. This also becomes critical when the need arises to escalate to your

leadership.

Escalation Dos and Don'ts

Escalations are often viewed as a bad thing, when in reality there are times when you need the leader's help to move your project along. An escalation can be an effective tool to bring awareness and help your project succeed. Here are some dos and don'ts when it comes to escalation.

Do:

- Escalate early.

- Be clear and concise in your messages.

- Give a heads up to those you are escalating on.

- Provide a solution to the problem with a timeline to resolve issues.

- State the facts.

- Give your resource a deadline and give them the opportunity to succeed. They need to know ahead of time that an escalation is forthcoming if the deadline is not met.

Don't

- Be accusatory

- Surprise your leadership with an escalation (leadership does not like surprises)

- Give a long winded explanation, even though you believe one is needed

- Send out an escalation before telling the resource being escalated on.

Pro Tip: Your project will typically not be the only thing your resources are responsible for. You will find they will react most to the "squeaky wheel". This is where your people skills will come into play so you can get them to focus them on the objectives to get your project done while being mindful of their other duties and responsibilities.

Closure

This is the part of the project where you formally close the project. By this time, the work is complete and has moved into an operational state. In this phase, you will release your resources and tie up any loose ends related to the project. This is also a good time to recognize your team members and highlight anyone who did outstanding work for you during the project.

Beyond Project Management

In this book, you've learned what a project

manager and the key skills needed to set you

apart from others in your field. You also

received some interview tips as well as some

Pro Tips to give you an edge in your career.

Whether you decide to make a career of project

management or have a desire to move into

people management, the skills and techniques

you have learned in this book will set you apart

from others, no matter which path you choose.

Take the time to continue to learn new skills

and create winning habits that will propel your

career to new heights. To learn more on

creating winning habits, you can click on the

following link and download my book *Habits:*

Create What You Need to Succeed in Life from Amazon. If you are looking to gain more comprehensive project management knowledge, I recommend you take an in person or online course on the subject. Also, you can purchase the Project Management Institute's book called the *Project Management Body of Knowledge* (PMBOK). This book contains knowledge contained in the Project Management Professional (PMP) and Certified Associate Project Management (CAPM) exams. For the requirements needed to take these exams, please visit the Project Management Institute.

Thank you!

I want to take a moment to say *Thank You* for reading this book and improving yourself. If this book was helpful for you, I would very much appreciate it if you'd go to Amazon and leave an honest review. I will have several books coming out over the next year, including books on Focus, Leadership, Intentions, Goals, and Thoughts. Your feedback will help me to create better books for you and help you reach your dreams and goals.

To stay in touch with me and learn when new books will be released, go to www.flight4success.com and join the FLIGHT crew. There you will have the opportunity for

beta reads and provide pre-launch book
feedback.

Until next time - Keep Reaching For New
Heights!

Your Friend,

Bryan

Glossary of Terms

The following is not a complete list but rather the most commonly used terms you will need to be familiar with as a project manager. For a full A-Z list you can visit Wikipedia.

Allocation is the assignment of available resources in an economic way.

Budget generally refers to a list of all planned expenses and revenues.

Change control is the procedures used to ensure that changes (normally, but not necessarily, to IT systems) are introduced in a controlled and coordinated manner. Change control is a major aspect of the broader discipline of change management.

Change management is a field of management focused on organizational changes. It aims to ensure that methods and procedures are used for efficient and prompt handling of all changes to controlled IT infrastructure, in order to minimize the number and impact of any related incidents upon service.

Critical path is the sequence of project network activities which add up to the longest overall duration, regardless if that longest duration has float or not. This determines the shortest time possible to complete the project.

Dependency in a project network is a link amongst a project's terminal elements.

Deliverable A contractually required work product, produced and delivered to a required state. A deliverable may be a document, hardware, software or other tangible product.

Gantt chart is a type of bar chart that illustrates a project schedule. It illustrates the start and finish dates of the terminal elements and summary elements of a project. Terminal elements and summary elements comprise the work breakdown structure of the project.

Issue – An error that has occurred during the course of a project that may affect the budget or schedule. Issues are typically tracked in an issue log.

Kickoff meeting is the first meeting with the project team and the client of the project.

Level of Effort (LOE) is qualified as a support type activity which doesn't lend itself to measurement of a discrete accomplishment. Examples of such an activity may be project budget accounting, customer liaison, etc.

Project plan is a formal, approved document used to guide both *project execution* and *project control*. The primary uses of the project plan are to document planning assumptions and decisions, facilitate communication among *stakeholders*, and document approved scope, cost, and schedule *baselines*. A project plan may be summary or detailed

Project team is the management team leading the project, and provide services to the project. Projects often bring together a variety number of problems. Stakeholders

have important issues with others

Resources are what is required to carry out a

project's tasks. They can be people,

equipment, facilities, funding, or anything else

capable of definition (usually other than labor)

required for the completion of a project activity

Risk is the precise probability of specific

eventualities.

Scope of a project in project management is

the sum total of all of its products and their

requirements or features

Tasks in project management are activity that

needs to be accomplished within a defined

period of time

Work Breakdown Structure (WBS) is a tool that defines a project and groups the project's discrete work elements in a way that helps organize and define the total work scope of the project. A Work breakdown structure element may be a product, data, a service, or any combination. WBS also provides the necessary framework for detailed cost estimating and control along with providing guidance for schedule development and control